CSB

I0468025

Hoeganaes Corporation: Gallatin, TN
Metal Dust Flash Fires and Hydrogen Explosion

January 31, 2011; March 29, 2011; May 27, 2011

5 Killed, 3 Injured

No. 2011-4-I-TN

KEY ISSUES
- Hazard recognition and training
- Engineering controls
- Fire codes/enforcement
- Regulatory oversight

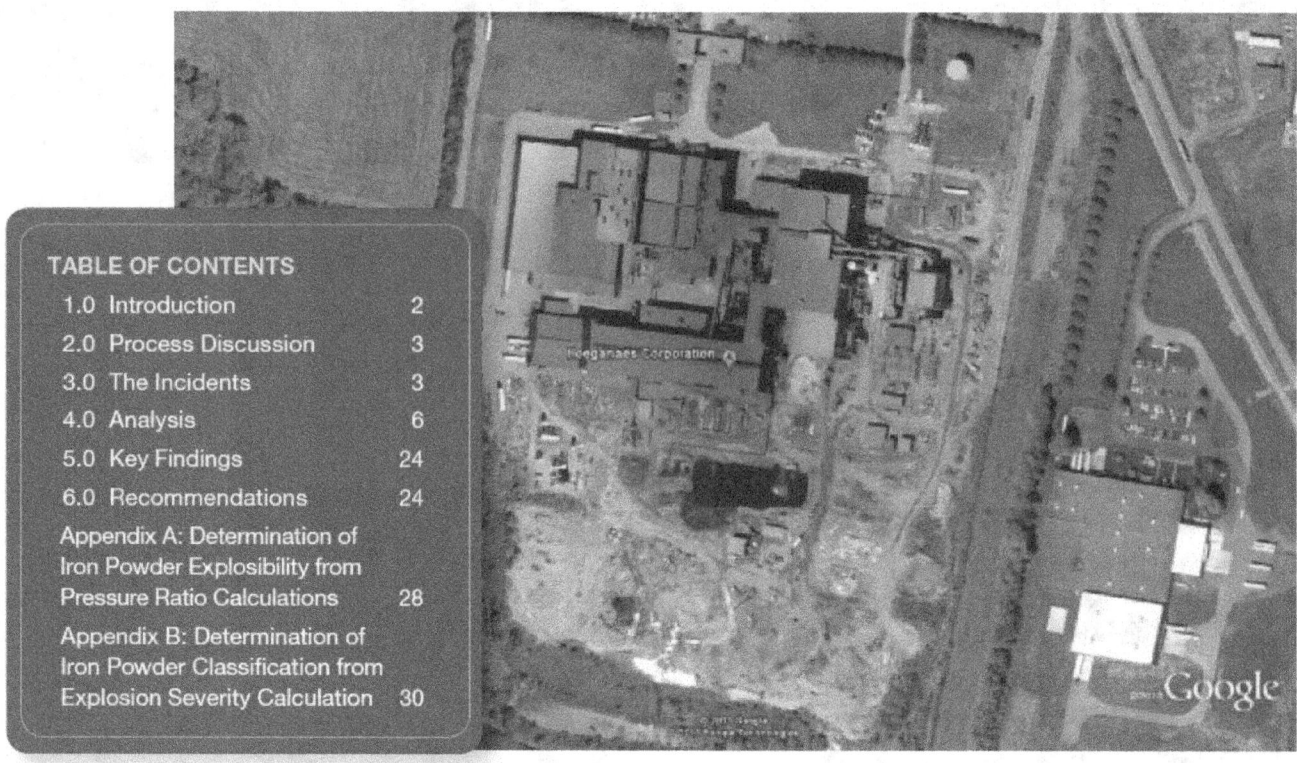

TABLE OF CONTENTS

1.0 Introduction	2
2.0 Process Discussion	3
3.0 The Incidents	3
4.0 Analysis	6
5.0 Key Findings	24
6.0 Recommendations	24
Appendix A: Determination of Iron Powder Explosibility from Pressure Ratio Calculations	28
Appendix B: Determination of Iron Powder Classification from Explosion Severity Calculation	30

FIGURE 1

Satellite view of the
Hoeganaes Gallatin facility.

1.0 INTRODUCTION

This case study examines multiple iron dust flash fires and a hydrogen explosion at the Hoeganaes facility in Gallatin, TN. The first iron dust flash fire incident killed two workers and the second injured an employee. The third incident, a hydrogen explosion and resulting iron dust flash fires, claimed three lives and injured two other workers.

1.1 HOEGANAES CORPORATION

Hoeganaes Corp. is a worldwide producer of atomized steel and iron powders. Headquartered in Cinnaminson, NJ, Hoeganaes has facilities in the U.S., Germany, China, and Romania.

The Hoeganaes Corp. is a subsidiary of GKN, a multinational engineering company headquartered in the United Kingdom. GKN has businesses in addition to powder metallurgy, including aerospace and automotive driveline industries. GKN acquired the Hoeganaes Corp. in 1999.

The largest consumer for the powdered metal (PM[1]) product is the automotive industry, which presses and sinters[2] the powder into small metal parts.

1.2 FACILITY DESCRIPTION

The Hoeganaes Gallatin facility (Figure 1), located 30 miles northeast of Nashville, Tennessee, employs just under 200 employees. Since becoming operational in the 1980s, they have increased their manufacturing capability over 550 percent from 45,000 to over 300,000 tons.

---

[1] PM is the accepted acronym by the powdered metals industry.

[2] Sintering is the process of solidifying PM via heat and/or pressure to form a component.

2.0 PROCESS DISCUSSION

Hoeganaes receives and melts scrap steel. Various elements are added to the molten metal to meet customer specifications, but the "workhorse" product, Ancorsteel 1000™, is over 99 percent iron. The molten iron is cooled and milled into a coarse powder that is processed in long annealing furnaces to make the iron more ductile.[3] The furnaces are called "band furnaces," for the 100 foot conveyor belt, or band, that runs through them. A hydrogen atmosphere is provided in the band furnace to reduce the iron by removing oxides and preventing oxidation. The hydrogen is supplied to the facility by a contract provider, onsite. Hydrogen is conveyed to the furnaces via pipes located in a trench under the floor and covered by metal plates.

In the process of going through the furnace, the coarse powder becomes a thick sheet called "cake." The cake is sent to a cake breaker and ultimately crushed into the fine PM product. The majority of the finished PM product has a particle diameter between 45-150 microns, or roughly the width of a human hair (Figure 2).

FIGURE 2

Fine PM collected from the Hoeganaes plant (penny shown for scale).

3.0 THE INCIDENTS

3.1 JANUARY 31, 2011 (TWO FATALITIES)

PM product is transferred through the plant by various mechanisms including screw conveyors and bucket elevators. Bucket elevators have a tendency to go "off-track" when the belt pulling the buckets becomes misaligned. Once sufficiently off-track the strain on the motor increases until the torque is too great and the motor shuts down. On January 31, 2011, at about 5:00 am Hoeganaes plant operators suspected bucket elevator #12 of being off-track and a maintenance mechanic and an electrician were called to inspect the equipment.

---

[3]Ductility is the physical property of a material where it is capable of sustaining large permanent changes in shape without breaking.

FIGURE 3 (LEFT)

Computer graphic of maintenance workers inspecting bucket elevator #12 just prior to January 31 flash fire.

FIGURE 4 (RIGHT)

Scene of January 31, 2011, incident area.

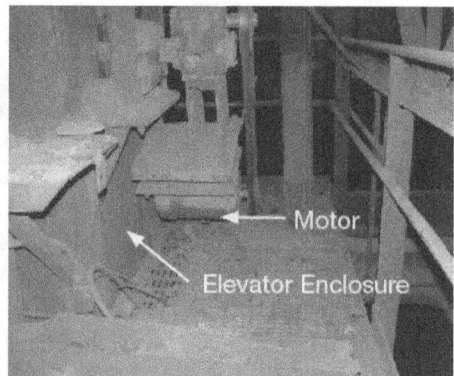

Based on their observations, they did not believe that the belt was off-track and requested, via radio, that the operator in the control room restart the motor (Figure 4). When the elevator was restarted, vibrations from the equipment dispersed fine iron dust into the air. During a CSB interview, one of the workers recalled being engulfed in flames, almost immediately after the motor was restarted.

FIGURE 5

Computer graphic of January 31 iron dust flash fire.

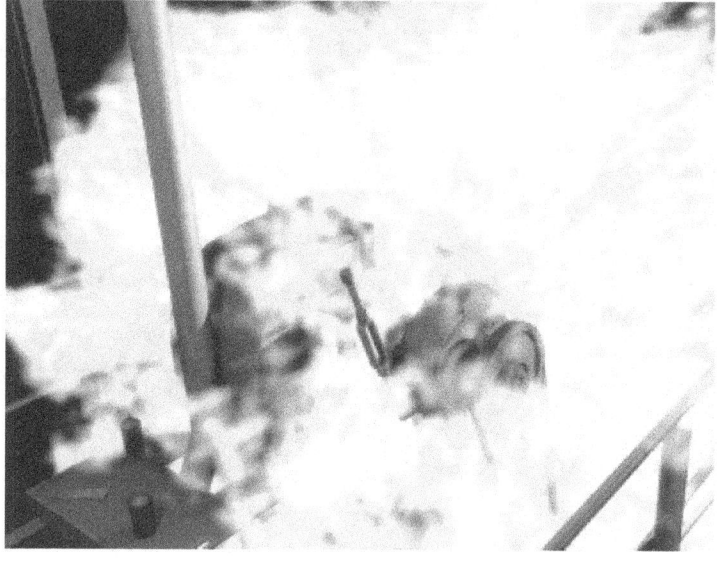

City of Gallatin emergency responders arrived with ambulances and transported the mechanic and electrician to the Vanderbilt Burn Center in Nashville, TN. Both employees were severely burned over a large percentage of their bodies. The first employee died from his injuries two days later. The second employee survived for nearly four months before succumbing to his injuries in late May 2011.

3.2 MARCH 29, 2011 (ONE INJURED)

As part of an ongoing furnace improvement project, a Hoeganaes engineer and an outside contractor were replacing igniters on a band furnace. The pair experienced difficulty in reconnecting a particular natural gas line after replacing an igniter. While using a hammer to force the gas port to reconnect, the Hoeganaes engineer inadvertently lofted large amounts of combustible iron dust from flat surfaces on the side of the band furnace, spanning 20 feet above him. As soon as the dust dispersed, the engineer recalled being engulfed in flames. He jumped and fell from a rolling stepladder in his attempt to escape the fireball. He received first- and second-degree burns to both thighs, superficial burns to his face, and scrapes from his fall. After seeing the initial flash of the dust igniting, the contractor took evasive action and escaped without injury.

FIGURE 6 (LEFT)

Computer graphic of
the gas line connection
involved in the March 29
flash fire.

FIGURE 7 (RIGHT)

The gas line connection
involved in March 29, 2011,
incident.

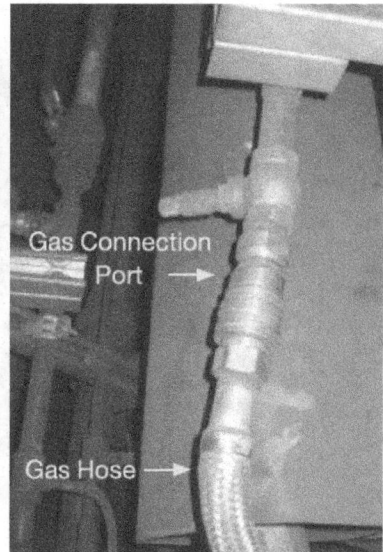

Gas Connection
Port →

Gas Hose →

FIGURE 8

Computer graphic of
March 29 iron dust
flash fire.

The engineer was wearing the Hoeganaes-designated personal protective equipment, which
included pants and a shirt that were rated as flame resistant clothing (FRC). He was also
wearing an FRC rated jacket that provided extra shielding to his upper torso from the flash
fire.

3.3 MAY 27, 2011 (THREE FATALITIES, TWO INJURIES)

Around 6 am on May 27, 2011, operators near band furnace #1 heard a hissing noise that
they identified as a gas leak. The operators determined that the leak was in a trench, an area
below the band furnaces that contains hydrogen, nitrogen, and cooling water runoff pipes,
in addition to a vent pipe for the furnaces. The operators informed the maintenance department about the hissing, and six mechanics were dispatched to find and repair the leak. One
annealing area operator stood by as the mechanics sought out the source of the leak.

Although maintenance personnel knew that hydrogen piping was in the same trench, they
presumed that the leak was nonflammable nitrogen because of a recent leak in a nitrogen
pipe elsewhere in the plant and began to try to remove trench covers. However, the trench

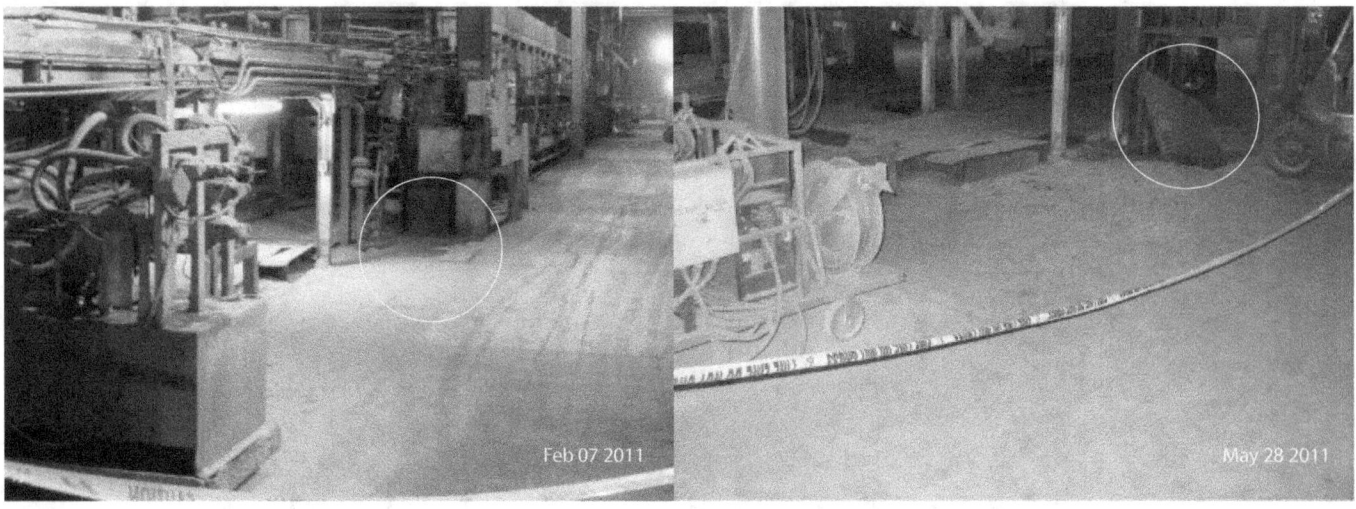

covers were too difficult to lift without machinery. Using an overhead crane, they were able to remove some of the trench covers. They determined that the leak was near the southernmost trench covers, which the crane could not reach. Shortly after 6:30 am, maintenance personnel acquired a forklift equipped with a chain on its forks, and were able to reach and begin removing the southernmost trench covers.

FIGURE 9 (TOP)

Scene of the May 27 incident before (left, taken during the CSB's January 31 incident investigation) and after (right). Note visible accumulations of iron powder on surfaces. Circled areas show trench cover location.

FIGURE 10 (RIGHT)

Computer graphic of maintenance crews starting to remove the trench covers using a forklift just prior to May 27 explosion.

Interviews with eyewitnesses indicate that just as the first trench cover was wrenched from its position by the forklift, friction created sparks, followed by a powerful explosion. Several days after the explosion, CSB investigators observed a large hole (approximately 3 x 7 inches) in a corroded section of piping that carried hydrogen and ran through the trench (Figure 11).

As the leaking hydrogen gas exploded, the resulting overpressure dispersed large quantities of iron dust from rafters and other surfaces in the upper reaches of the building. Portions of this dust subsequently ignited. Multiple eyewitnesses reported embers raining down and igniting

FIGURE 11 (TOP LEFT)

Hole in 4-inch piping after the May 27, 2011, incident.

FIGURE 12 (TOP RIGHT)

Computer graphic of the May 27, 2011, hydrogen explosion.

FIGURE 13 (BOTTOM)

Upward disturbance of trench covers caused by the hydrogen explosion in the May 27, 2011, incident.

multiple dust flash fires in the area. They also reported visibility so limited in some instances that flashlights were required; one eyewitness said that even with a flashlight, he could see only 3 to 4 feet ahead due to extensive dust and smoke.

The hydrogen explosion and ensuing iron dust flash fires injured four of the responding mechanics and the annealing operator.[4] The two mechanics near the forklift were transported to a local hospital where they were treated for smoke inhalation and released shortly thereafter.

Two other mechanics and the operator who stood by during the operation were rushed to Vanderbilt Burn Center. Less than a week after the incident, two employees succumbed to their injuries. The third seriously injured employee died from his injuries almost seven weeks after the incident.

Due to the extensive nature of the injuries, and the abundance of both hydrogen and combustible dust present at the time of the incident, it is difficult to specifically determine which fuel, if not both, caused the fatal injuries to the victims.

3.4 EMERGENCY RESPONSE

The Gallatin Fire Department (GFD) has responded to 30 incidents of various types over the past 12 years at the Hoeganaes Corp., including the January 31, March 29, and May 27 incidents. In June 1999, the GFD responded to a fire caused by iron dust that ignited in a baghouse. One person suffered smoke inhalation injuries as a result of the incident.

Before the GFD arrived at each of the 2011 incidents, Hoeganaes volunteer first responders cared for the injured. Hoeganaes volunteers participate in annual training that covers first response, CPR, and first aid. They are instructed to provide care until GFD and EMS responders arrive.

Immediately following each incident, the volunteers provided first aid and comfort to the injured by applying water to cool the burns and covering the victims with a burn blanket to keep them comfortable. EMS arrived within minutes of the initial 9-1-1 call and transported the injured personnel to hospitals.

---

[4]At the time of incident, two of the mechanics and the operator were standing near the trench while the other two mechanics were positioned and possibly shielded by the forklift when the explosion occurred.

4.0 ANALYSIS

4.1 COMBUSTIBLE DUST TESTING

According to National Fire Protection Association (NFPA) 484, *Standard for Combustible Metals*, a facility that handles metal dust should commission one of two screening tests to determine if a metal dust is combustible and the provisions of the standard apply (Section 4.4.1). If results from either of the two tests show that the dust is combustible or explosible, NFPA 484 would apply to the facility either as a matter of voluntary good practice or as a requirement by a relevant regulatory body.

The first screening test for the determination of combustibility, also known as the "train test," measures the burning rate of a dust layer over the length of a sample.[5] If there is propagation beyond the ignition point or heated zone, then the sample is considered combustible.[6]

The second test, for explosibility determination, serves as a basis to determine if a metal powder or dust is capable of initiating an explosion when suspended in a dust cloud. This test, performed in a Hartmann apparatus, determines the minimum ignition energy of a dust cloud in air by a high voltage spark.[7]

If either of the screening tests produces a positive result for combustibility or explosibility, NFPA 484 requires further explosibility testing be conducted in a 20-L sphere. Several values (below) from the explosibility test results can be used to characterize the severity of a dust explosion.

EXPLOSIVITY VALUES

K_{St}: calculated value that compares the relative explosion severity and consequence to other dusts (bar m/s). The higher the K_{St} number, the more energetic the explosion.

P_{max}: maximum explosion overpressure generated in the test vessel (bar)

$\partial P / \partial t$: maximum rate of pressure rise, predicts violence of the explosion (bar/s)

Explosion Severity (ES): Index to determine if Class II electrical equipment is required as an OSHA requirement.

ES > 0.5, Class II Combustible
ES < 0.4, Combustible but not Class II

4.1.1 CSB COMBUSTIBLE DUST TESTING

4.1.1.1 Combustibility Demonstration

In order to visually demonstrate the combustibility of the Hoeganaes iron samples, a modified "Go/No-Go" test was performed by the CSB. Generally, this test is performed in a closed vessel, but the CSB was interested in directly observing any flames the dust may produce.[8]

---

[5]UN Recommendations on the Transport of Dangerous Goods: Model Regulations – Manual of Tests and Criteria, Part III, Subsection 33.2.1

[6]NFPA 484 defines a combustible metal dust as a particulate metal that presents a fire or explosion hazard when suspended in air or the process specific oxidizing medium over a range of concentrations, regardless of particle size or shape.

[7]ASTM E2019, Standard Test Method for Minimum Ignition Energy of a Dust Cloud in Air

[8]The "Go/No-Go" test is typically performed in a modified one-liter Hartmann tube; also known as the explosibility screening test as described in NFPA 484.

This test dispersed about 30 grams of iron dust—sampled from the baghouse[9] associated with the bucket elevator from the January 31, 2011, incident—above an 8 inch burner. Upon being released, the dust auto-ignites in air due to the heat given off from the burner below (Figure 14). An intense white flame was produced that reached a peak diameter of 18 inches.

FIGURE 14

CSB iron dust
combustibility
demonstration, see
Section 4.1.1.1.

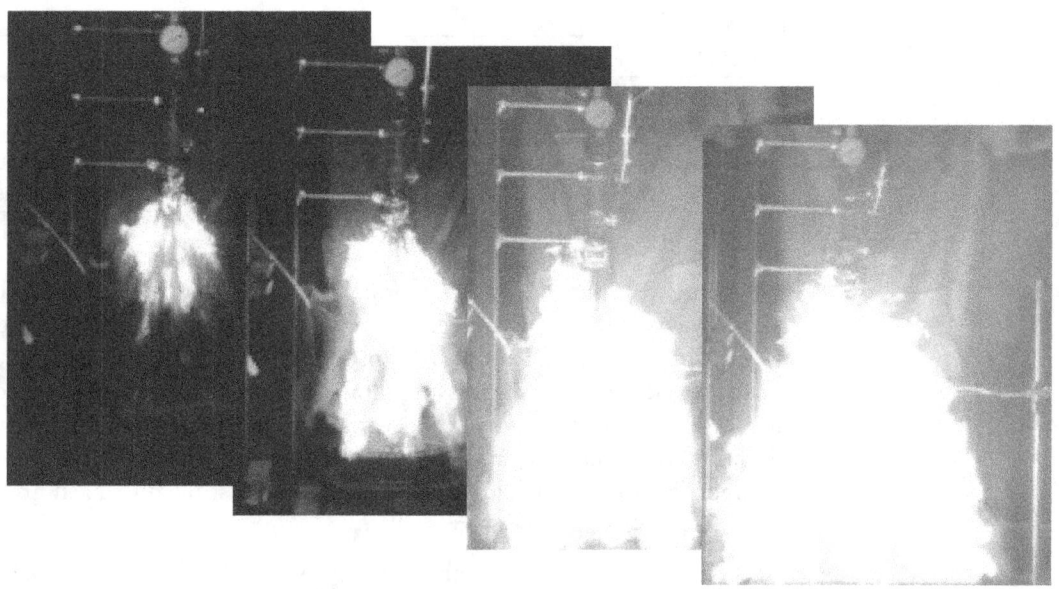

4.1.1.2 20-Liter (20-L) Test Method

CSB investigators collected iron powder samples from various locations in the Hoeganaes facility and commissioned testing to characterize its combustibility using two different test methods, the 20-liter (20-L) and one-meter cubed (1-m^3) test chambers. The 20-L test laboratory used the standard test method, ASTM E1226, *Pressure and Rate of Pressure Rise for Combustible Dusts*, for the selected iron powder samples. Each dust sample was injected and ignited in a 20-L spherical test vessel equipped with transducers to record a pressure-versus-time profile of the dust deflagration in the sphere.

Table 1 shows data from the CSB's combustibility tests of the Hoeganaes dust and a comparison to dust testing the CSB commissioned for previous dust incidents at other companies.

The CSB test data indicate that the iron powder is combustible and is covered by the requirements of NFPA 484 (Section 4.4.1). Although values indicate that the dust produces a weak explosion relative to other dusts, the dust is considered combustible by the OSHA definition[10] and can result in a flash fire capable of causing injuries and fatalities.

[9]Ventilation equipment that removes airborne particulate by forcing air through a specially designed filtration bag.

[10]OSHA 3371-08 2009: "a solid material composed of distinct particles or pieces, regardless of size, shape, or chemical composition, which presents a fire or deflagration hazard when suspended in air or some other oxidizing medium over a range of concentrations."

TABLE 1

Combustibility data for selected materials.

20-L COMBUSTIBLE DUST TEST DATA FROM CSB INVESTIGATIONS[11]					
	Hoeganaes Iron Dust 20L test[12]	Granulated Sugar	Aluminum Dust	Polyethylene Dust	Phenolic Resin
P_{max} (bar)	3.5	5.2	9.4	8.34	7.58
$\partial P/\partial t$ (bar/s)	68	129	357	515	586
K_{St} (bar m/s)	19	35	103	140	165
Explosion Severity (ES)	0.077	0.22	1.08	1.38	1.43
Classification	Combustible	Combustible	Combustible, Class II	Combustible, Class II	Combustible, Class II

Frequently, the hazards of different combustible dusts are evaluated by their potential explosive capabilities. However, the hazards of combustible dusts are not limited to explosions. The Hoeganaes iron powder propagates an explosion less rapidly compared to other dusts, so there is less overpressure damage, consistent with observations by CSB investigators. Dust testing results from Hoeganaes and prior CSB investigations illustrate that dusts with low K_{St} values can cause flash fires that result in deaths and serious injuries. Although combustible dusts can lead to explosions, combustible dust flash fires also pose a risk that must be addressed in industry.

According to the 20-L standard test method, E1226, a dust sample can be defined as combustible or explosible based on a calculated pressure ratio (PR) using the pressure data recorded in the 20-L test chamber. For sample concentrations of 1,000 and 2,000 g/m³, a pressure ratio value greater than or equal to 2 is considered explosible. If the pressure ratio is less than 2, the sample is considered non-explosible. However, the test method cautions that the dust can still burn and a dust cloud may experience a deflagration depending upon conditions such as the temperature and particle size.[13] The iron dust sample from baghouse #4 had a PR of 4.0 and 4.7 at concentrations of 1,000 and 2,000 g/m³ respectively, indicating that the dust sample is explosible.

4.1.1.3 One-Meter Cubed (1-m³) Test Method

The CSB collected a subsequent sample[14] from baghouse #4 and subjected it to combustibility testing using the one-meter cubed (1-m³) method, ISO 6184-1 *Explosion Protection Systems: Determination of Explosion Indices of Combustible Dusts in Air*. The 1-m³ test vessel is larger than the 20-L vessel, and the dust, along with air and a fuel source, is injected into the system differently.

The iron powder from baghouse #4 underwent an explosibility screening test in the 1-m³ vessel in an attempt to ignite the sample. At several dust concentrations, none of the tests produced significant pressure which exceeded the test qualifications for ignition and therefore the dust sample was considered non-explosible according to this method.

---

[11]For a more detailed discussion on characteristic combustible dust values, see CSB 2006-H-1 *Combustible Dust Hazard Study.*

[12]CSB investigators collected this iron dust sample from baghouse #4 at the Hoeganaes Gallatin facility after the January 31, 2011, incident.

[13]American Society for Testing and Materials (ASTM), E1226-10, *Pressure and Rate of Pressure Rise for Combustible Dust*, ASTM International, 2010.

[14]At the time this sample was taken in August 2011, the Gallatin facility had not been fully operational for about three months. As such, the sample collected did not contain fines representative of the environment at the time of the 2011 flash fire incidents.

4.1.1.4 Comparing Dust Testing Methods

Both the 20-L and 1-m^3 tests are accepted methods that can characterize dust explosibility; however results from the two tests may differ. There are several factors that can contribute to varying results among the dust test methods. Dust characteristics, such as particle size, moisture content, and degree of oxidation (for metals) can affect the ignitability of the sample in the test chamber.

The 20-L and 1-m^3 test chambers were designed to simulate dust explosions in facility settings, but each test has limitations. The main difference between the two tests is the chamber size and the dust dispersion mechanism. Since the 1-m^3 test is larger, theoretically it can better simulate an open-space dust cloud explosion. However, that larger volume also makes it harder to create a uniform distribution of dust within the testing chamber. In the smaller 20-L test chamber it is easier to create a uniform distribution; however, it is possible that the smaller chamber also creates an "overdriving" effect. Since the 20-L chamber is smaller, the energy exerted by the igniters[15] may combust enough dust creating the appearance of ignition[16] — a situation that would not occur in a facility setting.

NFPA revised the 2012 edition of NFPA 484 to state that explosibility screening tests shall be performed in accordance to the 20-L test standard, E1226. However, NFPA added to the standard annex that the results of the 20-L test can be conservative and an owner or operator of a facility may elect to use a 1-m^3 test for dust explosibility testing as the 20-L test may result in false positives for dusts with lower K_{St} values.

Despite the discrepancies between the two test methods, the empirical evidence from the flash fire incidents at Hoeganaes shows that dusts with lower K_{St} values are capable of fueling flash fires with severe consequences. This further suggests that facilities should not rely on the 1-m^3 test as a sole determination of dust combustibility hazards. Dusts with lower K_{St} values and characteristics similar to the iron powder at Hoeganaes may not ignite in the 1-m^3 chamber but still have the ability to result in fatal flash fires.

It should be noted that both tests are for *explosibility* screening, and alone may not convey the full *combustibility* hazard.

4.1.2 HOEGANAES COMBUSTIBLE DUST TESTING

4.1.2.1 Minimum Ignition Energy (MIE)

In 2010, Hoeganaes contracted to test iron dust samples from the plant for combustibility as a result of an insurance audit recommendation. The test had one sample that was similar in particle size, moisture content, and location to the dust involved in the 2011 incidents. That sample gave the results seen in Table 2.

The minimum ignition energy (MIE) testing determined that a continuous arc did ignite the representative samples from 2010, but a 500 mJ source did not. The conclusion from the testing was that the minimum ignition energy was greater than 500 mJ. This information is valuable in determining potential ignition sources for each of the incidents.

---

[15]The igniter may increase the temperature in the smaller 20-L chamber, raising the overall temperature of the system and allowing a non-explosive system to appear explosive.

[16]Going, J et al., "Flammability limit measurements for dust in 20-L and 1-m^3 vessels." *Journal of Loss Prevention in the Process Industries.* May 2003

TABLE 2

Combustible dust test results commissioned by Hoeganaes in 2010.

HOEGANAES MINIMUM IGNITION ENERGY (MIE) TEST RESULTS	
Sample	Iron Dust
Particle size (%<75 μm)	99%
P_{max} (bar)	3.3
$(\partial P/\partial t)_{max}$ (bar/s)	51
K_{st} (bar*m/s)	15
MIE (mJ[17], Cloud)	>500
MIT[18] (°C, Cloud)	560-580
MEC[19] (g/m³)	200-250

4.2 IGNITION SOURCES

Witnesses indicated that the May 27, 2011, hydrogen explosion was ignited by sparks generated during the lifting of the trench cover. This is reasonable considering that the MIE of hydrogen is 0.02 mJ, and the energy of mechanical sparks from metal to metal contact can be several mJ.[20]

FIGURE 15

Exposed electrical wiring on elevator motor near January 2011 incident site (motor panel cover was rotated post incident by fire department).

The testing contracted by Hoeganaes in 2010 determined that the minimum ignition energy for representative iron dust samples was greater than 500 mJ, and that a continuous arc would ignite the samples. One witness at ground level reported hearing an "electric sound" at the time of the incident. The motor operating bucket elevator #12 was a likely source of ignition since it had exposed wiring, was not properly grounded, and was within a few feet of the dust cloud source. The wiring was exposed because the electrical conduit supplying power to this motor was not securely connected to the motor's junction box.

---

[17]mJ is an abbreviation for millijoules, which is a unit of energy. One Joule is equal to 1000 millijoules or approximately 0.24 calorie.

[18]Minimum Ignition Temperature.

[19]Minimum Explosible Concentration.

[20]V. Babrauskas, Ignition Handbook, Fire Science Publishers, Issaquah, WA, 2003.

Prior to the CSB notifying Hoeganaes that evidence from the incident area needed to be preserved, the company removed and modified evidence from the scene, including the elevator motor, wiring, and conduit. However, on examination, there were spots that appeared to be arc marks both inside the junction box, and on the outside of the motor housing.

4.3 HOEGANAES

4.3.1 HAZARD RECOGNITION

FIGURE 16

Mounds of iron dust along elevated surfaces at the Gallatin plant, February 3, 2011.

In general industry the combustibility of metal dust is a well-established hazard, but metal dust fires and explosions continue to claim lives and destroy property. The CSB reviewed three publications dating back to the 1940s and 1950s that addressed metal dust (including iron dust) hazards and explosion protection methods. The National Fire Protection Association (NFPA) code for the Prevention of Dust Explosions, published in 1946,[21] lists general precautions for all types of dusts, including metal powder, and specific provisions for certain types of dusts.

The Building Construction section of the code states, "Avoid beams, ledges or other places where dust may settle, particularly overhead." The Gallatin facility, built in the 1980s, was not designed to avoid significant overhead accumulations of dust. The code calls for designing and maintaining dust-tight equipment to avoid leaks and, where this is not possible, to enforce good housekeeping procedures.

The code also cautions against sources of ignition in areas containing dust and recommends locating dust collectors outdoors or in separate rooms equipped with explosion venting.

In 1957, the NFPA published the *Report of Important Dust Explosions* which included a summary of over 1,000 dust explosions between 1860 and 1956 in the U.S. and Canada.[22] The report listed 80 metal dust fires and explosions, including one iron dust incident that resulted in a fatality in 1951.

A 1958 article in an American Chemical Society publication states, "Powdered metals dispersed in oxygen or air form explosive mixtures... their flammability and explosibility have been reported in considerable detail..."[23]

---

[21]National Fire Codes, Vol. II. The Prevention of Dust Explosions 1946. National Fire Protection Association, Boston, MA., 1946.

[22]National Fire Protection Association, *Report of Important Dust Explosions*, NFPA, Boston, MA, 1950.

[23]Grosse, A.V., and J.B. Conway. "Combustion of Metals in Oxygen." *Industrial & Engineering Chemistry* 50.4 (1958): 663-72.

In the 1990s and 2000s, the Pittsburgh Research Laboratory of the National Institute for Occupational Safety and Health (NIOSH) conducted a study of the explosibility of various metals, including iron. The results of these experiments, published in scientific journals,[24] showed the explosibility characteristics of iron powder to aid hazard evaluation in metal processing industries. However, management within the Hoeganaes Corp. and GKN Corp. did not commission an analysis of its own potentially combustible PM products and constituents until January 2009, as a result of an insurance audit conducted in 2008. This combustible dust testing concluded that all three iron powder samples collected from various locations in the plant were explosible (Section 4.3.6.1). However, these results did not trigger an effective overhaul of the dust containment and housekeeping procedures at the Gallatin facility.

Representatives from Hoeganaes told the CSB that the dust analysis results did trigger an operator training program for the recognition of combustible dust hazards. However, Hoeganaes did not mitigate the dust hazard. Since Hoeganaes did not control the combustible dust hazard, operators were forced to tolerate the conditions at the facility. Over time, these flash fires became normalized, since they did not result in any serious injuries prior to the fatal incident on January 31, 2011.

Operators and mechanics reported being involved in multiple flash fires during their employment at the Gallatin facility. At the time of the incidents, many were aware that the iron dust could burn or smolder. However, they were not trained to understand the potentially severe hazard when accumulated dust is dispersed in air. Rarely would operators report the minor flash fires and near-misses that periodically occurred.

4.3.2 ENGINEERING CONTROLS

4.3.2.1 Combustible Dust

Thorough hazard recognition is key to effectively managing the risk from combustible dust. Once the hazard is recognized, applying the "hierarchy of controls" for fire and explosion prevention helps address the fugitive dust issue at the source: the material itself, the processing equipment, and the work procedures. The hierarchy of controls is a safety concept in which a hierarchal ordering of control mechanisms is applied to reduce risk. It covers the spectrum from elimination at the source, at the top of the hierarchy, through engineering and administrative (procedural) controls to personal protective equipment (PPE), at the bottom of the hierarchy.[25]

Installing and maintaining engineering controls to eliminate fugitive dust accumulation is the most effective method to prevent dust fires and explosions. Conveyance systems and appropriately sized dust collection equipment are examples of engineering controls that eliminate or mitigate fugitive dust generation at the source. Engineering controls are preferred over housekeeping, but a robust housekeeping program is important to manage fugitive dust accumulations in areas where engineering controls need maintenance or improvement. Additionally, administrative controls, such as worker training and operating procedures, complement robust engineering controls.

Significant quantities of iron dust escaped from equipment throughout the Hoeganaes facility. Enclosures on the conveyance equipment leaked fugitive emissions of iron dust.. In addition, the dust collection systems were historically unreliable and did not prevent large amounts of combustible iron dust from becoming airborne and accumulating on elevated surfaces throughout the processing areas.

[24]Cashdollar, K., Flammability of Metals and Other Elemental Dust Clouds. Loss Prevention Symposium. AICHE 1994.
  Cashdollar, K., Zlochower, I., Explosion Temperatures and Pressures of Metals and other Elemental Dust Clouds. Journal of Loss Prevention in the Process Industries 20 (337-348) 2007.

[25]Kletz, T., Amyotte, P., *Process Plants: A Handbook for Inherently Safer Design*. CRC Press, 2010.

4.3.2.2 Hydrogen

The trench involved on the May 27, 2011, incident contains many pipes including nitrogen and hydrogen supply and vent pipes for the band furnaces. In addition to housing pipes, the trench also acts as a drain for the cooling water used in the band furnaces. At the time of the incident this water came out of the furnaces hot and drained directly onto the pipes and into the trench (Figure 17).

FIGURE 17

Water flow (upper left of photo) and externally corroded pipes in the trench involved in the May 27, 2011, incident.

STANDARDS THAT ADDRESS THE HYDROGEN SUPPLY AND VENT PIPES IN THE TRENCH INCLUDE:

- ASME[26] B31.3, Process Piping
- CGA[27] G-5.4-2010, Standard for Hydrogen Piping Systems at User Locations
- NFPA 2, Hydrogen Technologies Code
- NFPA 55, Compressed Gases and Cryogenic Fluids Code.

According to ASME B31.3, design concerns about ambient conditions around process pipes focus on environments and changes that can create physical stresses in the piping. Section 10.5.3 of NFPA 55 requires annual maintenance including inspection for physical damage and leak tightness. CGA G-5.4 similarly requires regular inspection for physical damage and leak tightness. However, Hoeganaes did not regularly inspect the pipes in the trench. The design and maintenance of this trench, should have addressed the issue of slow corrosion over time caused by the hot water runoff and solids accumulation.

Both NFPA 55 and NFPA 2 state, "Provisions shall be made for controlling and mitigating unauthorized discharges." NFPA 2 further requires that "the storage, use, or handling of [hydrogen] in a building or facility shall be accomplished in a manner that provides a reasonable level of safety... from illness, injury or death..." However, the CSB found no evidence of a Hoeganaes procedure to inspect piping within the trench to ensure that corrosion had not compromised the piping systems which would allow an uncontrolled release of hydrogen. Moreover, Hoeganaes had no written procedure or protocol to mitigate gas leaks, and maintenance crews were allowed to begin investigating a suspected leak without testing the atmosphere for concentrations of explosive gas.

4.3.3 ADMINISTRATIVE CONTROLS

4.3.3.1 Housekeeping

Observations by CSB investigators at the Gallatin facility shortly after the first incident indicated that combustible dust was leaking from equipment and that housekeeping was ineffective (see Figures 16, 18, 19, 20 and 21). Combustible iron dust coated almost every

---

[26]The American Society of Mechanical Engineers (ASME) is a professional body focused on mechanical engineering. The organization is known for setting codes and standards for mechanical devices. The ASME conducts one of the world's largest technical publishing operations through the ASME Press. The organization holds numerous technical conferences and hundreds of professional development courses each year, and sponsors numerous outreach and educational programs.

[27]The Compressed Gas Association (CGA) develops and publishes technical information, standards, and recommendations for the manufacture, storage, transportation, distribution, and use of industrial gases.

Iron dust on rafters,
February 3, 2011.

Iron dust on overhead
surfaces, February 3, 2011.

surface up to 4 inches deep and was visible in the air. Mitigation of the combustible dust hazard by Hoeganaes was limited to a less-than-adequate vacuuming service, sparsely enclosed conveyance equipment, and an inadequate baghouse filtration system.

Although bucket elevators and some conveyance equipment were enclosed, fugitive dust emissions were evident throughout the facility. Moreover, the CSB investigators observed leaks of fugitive dust to the atmosphere when the bags used in the baghouse filtration system were pulsed, which allowed dust to escape into the work areas many times each hour. The baghouse filters are designed to collect the smallest, and consequently most dangerous, dust particles. Yet, the CSB found that the baghouses were often out of service. Employees reported that the baghouse associated with bucket elevator #12 was out of service sporadically for the 7 days leading up to the fatal incident on January 31, 2011, allowing fine combustible iron dust to remain in the area, from which it was dispersed when the elevator was restarted during maintenance.

Iron dust on structural
supports, February 3, 2011.

4.3.4 PERSONAL PROTECTIVE EQUIPMENT

4.3.4.1 Flame Resistant Clothing (FRC)

Workers in production-related operations wear flame resistant clothing (FRC) to reduce risk of thermal injury from flash fire incidents. As part of the Personal Protective Equipment (PPE) Standard (29 CFR 1910.132), OSHA requires employers to provide workers with FRC in workplaces when flash fire or explosion hazards are present.

FRC can reduce the severity of burn injuries sustained during a flash fire when engineering and administrative controls fail. FRC, usually worn as coveralls, is made of treated natural or synthetic fibers that resist burning and withstand heat.

There are two NFPA standards that provide guidance on the design and use of FRC. NFPA 2112, *Standard on Flame-Resistant Garments for Protection of Industrial Personnel Against Flash Fire*, provides the minimum requirements for the design, testing, and certification of FRC. NFPA 2113, *Standard on Selection, Care, Use, and Maintenance of Flame-Resistant Garments for the Protection of Industrial Personnel Against Flash Fire*, provides guidance for the selection, use, and maintenance of FRC. The 2009 edition of NFPA 484 included a requirement for workers to wear FRC if working in metal dust-handling operations, but it did not specifically reference NFPA 2112 or 2113 in the standard. The 2012 edition of NFPA 484 requires that new and existing facilities covered by the standard adhere to the requirements of NFPA 2113 for FRC.

Hoeganaes employees were required to wear FRC, and the injured and fatally injured employees were wearing the Hoeganaes-designated FRC at the time of the 2011 flash fire incidents. Though FRC is intended to reduce the severity of thermal injuries, five severely burned employees died following the January and May incidents. The specific FRC worn did not provide any significant protection against the combustible iron dust flash fires and the hydrogen explosion at Hoeganaes.

4.3.5 1992 INCIDENT

On May 13, 1992, a hydrogen explosion and iron dust flash fire similar to the May 2011 incident in Gallatin severely burned an employee working at the Hoeganaes facility in Cinnaminson, NJ. CSB investigators interviewed the injured employee from the 1992 incident and learned that a hydrogen explosion event in a furnace dispersed and ignited significant accumulations of iron dust which resulted in thermal burns over 90% of his body. The injured worker spent a year in a burn unit and is still recovering from his burn injuries.

4.3.6 INSURANCE INSPECTIONS

4.3.6.1 Allianz

TABLE 3

Dust explosibility test results commissioned by Hoeganaes in 2009.

HOEGANAES IRON DUST EXPLOSIBILITY TESTING			
(20-L)			
Sample	Base Iron	Furnace Feed	Baghouse Dust
P_{max} (bar)	1.9	2.8	3.8
$\partial P/\partial t$ (bar/s)	273	63	80
K_{St} (bar m/s)	74	17	22

In November 2008, Allianz, a German-based risk insurer, conducted a routine audit of the Hoeganaes facility. The audit report noted that improved housekeeping was needed in several areas of the facility. In the list of risk improvement proposals, the Allianz report stated, "The potential for explosions caused when clouds of powdered metal are aroused in equipment... should be analyzed by an independent consultant." The proposal recommended an independent dust hazard analysis and a subsequent hazard study to identify suitable mitigation techniques, should the iron dust in the facility be found to be explosible.

In January 2009, Hoeganaes collected samples of base iron dust, furnace-feed dust, and baghouse dust and commissioned explosibility testing as Allianz recommended (Table 3). In September 2010, Hoeganaes requested another test of various powdered metals. Test results showed that 5 of the 9 iron samples had K_{St} values greater than 1.

The Allianz audit findings initiated several action items as part of the Hoeganaes Combustible Dust Program at the Gallatin facility. The scope of the program was to understand and align company practices with the OSHA Combustible Dust National Emphasis Program (NEP) (Section 4.5.1). Action items included combustible dust training for employees and understanding relevant NFPA codes at the facility. Although the majority of the Hoeganaes Combustible Dust Program action items had planned completion dates prior to the 2011 flash fire incidents, the program did not effectively mitigate the combustible dust hazards at the facility.

4.4 FIRE CODES

4.4.1 NFPA 484

NFPA 484, *Standard for Combustible Metals*, an industry consensus standard, applies to facilities that produce, process, finish, handle, recycle, and store metals and alloys in a form capable of combustion or explosion. NFPA codes involving combustible metal dusts have evolved several times since the 1946 *The Prevention of Dust Explosions* (Section 4.3.1). In the 1950s, the NFPA divided the 1946 document into several codes for specific materials, such as magnesium and titanium. In 2002, all of the NFPA combustible metal dust standards were combined into NFPA 484. NFPA 484 describes the tests and methods for determining metal dust combustibility and provides guidelines for preventing dust explosions and flash fires for all types of metal dusts.

The CSB commissioned testing similar to the 2009 edition of NFPA 484 explosibility determination test requirements (Section 4.1). The testing concluded that the Hoeganaes metal dust sample is explosible and therefore NFPA 484 applies.

Had Hoeganaes voluntarily followed, or been required to follow, NFPA 484 by the GFD (authority having jurisdiction[28]) the January and March incidents may have been prevented, and the effects of the May accident could have been reduced. As with many NFPA standards, NFPA 484 has a retroactivity clause for certain chapters, stating that requirements for all existing equipment, installed prior to the current edition of the code, are not enforceable by the authority having jurisdiction, unless it is determined that the existing situation presents an unacceptable safety and health hazard.

FIGURE 21

Photo of equipment obscured by airborne dust, taken by CSB investigators, February 7, 2011.

Neither the City of Gallatin nor the GFD identified combustible metal dust as a concern or hazard during previous inspections conducted prior to the 2011 incidents (Section 4.4.3).

Chapter 12 of NFPA 484, "Requirements for Combustible Metals" includes provisions to control or eliminate dust fires and explosions. It requires engineering controls for dust-producing processes such as enclosures and capture devices connected to dust collection systems. The standard describes recommended housekeeping practices and frequencies, and how to control ignition sources.

Practices at Hoeganaes did not conform to the safety recommendations set forth in NFPA 484. Under "Building Construction," NFPA 484 requires that floors, elevated platforms, and gratings where dust can accumulate be designed to minimize dust accumulations and facilitate cleaning.[29] The Hoeganaes facility has numerous flat surfaces overhead upon which the CSB investigators observed significant accumulations of combustible iron dust. Since Hoeganaes has an iron powder-producing operation, specific engineering controls outlined in NFPA 484 apply to the machines that manufacture and convey the PM. All machines that produce fine particles of iron should be connected to a dust collection system that has the appropriate velocity to capture all dust. The CSB investigators observed that some of the PM conveyance equipment at

---

[28]The organization, office, or individual responsible for approving equipment, materials, an installation, or a procedure.

[29]Chapter 12 is not retroactive to existing facilities.

Hoeganaes's was not enclosed; as such, it was not designed to control significant dust emissions, and employees further reported that baghouse dust collectors were often down for maintenance. This section of the standard also requires that dust collection systems be located outdoors; at Hoeganaes, the baghouses are located inside, posing a serious fire and explosion hazard.

Chapter 13 of NFPA 484 includes provisions for housekeeping and applies to all new and existing facilities. It requires that accumulations of excessive dust on any portions of buildings or machinery not regularly cleaned in daily operations be minimized and that fugitive dust not be allowed to accumulate. Hoeganaes used a vacuuming service to reduce quantities of dust that had accumulated. However, inadequate dust collection systems and dust leakages from equipment produced accumulations beyond what could be controlled by the limited housekeeping service that was being provided.

4.4.2 ELECTRICAL CLASSIFICATION

The classification of combustible dust hazardous locations is based on the criteria established by article 500 of NFPA 70, *National Electric Code* (NEC). The NEC defines hazardous locations as areas "where fire or explosion hazards may exist due to flammable gases or vapors, flammable liquids, combustible dust, or ignitable fibers or flyings." The classifications are broken down into three hazardous material classes:

- Class I – flammable gas or vapor
- Class II – combustible dust
- Class III – fibers and flyings

Each class is further categorized into one of two divisions, based on operating conditions:

- Division 1 – Normal: areas where the classified hazardous material is likely to be present under normal operating conditions
- Division 2 – Abnormal: areas where the classified hazardous material is likely to be contained and present only through accidental release

With the proper evaluation of electrically classified areas in an operating facility, appropriately rated equipment can be installed.

4.4.2.1 Combustible Dust

NFPA 499, *Classification of Combustible Dusts and of Hazardous (Classified) Locations for Electrical Installation in Chemical Process Areas*, specifies the type of electrical equipment acceptable in atmospheres containing combustible dust. It applies to locations where combustible dusts are produced, processed, and handled, or where surface accumulations of dust could be ignited by electrical equipment. Based on the requirements of NFPA 499 and the NEC, classified electric services and equipment would be required in a facility where combustible metal dust was present. Specifically, NFPA 499 states that Division 1 electrical equipment should be used in areas where combustible dust can accumulate to 1/8 of an inch (3 mm).

OSHA 1910 Subpart S includes definitions and requirements for hazardous or electrically classified locations. To determine whether classified electrical equipment is needed for a combustible dust, a Class II combustibility test is conducted with dust samples from the facility and the explosion severity (ES) ratio calculated. An ES of greater than 0.5 signifies an appreciable explosion hazard, which means either that Class II electrical equipment must be installed or dust accumulations near electrical equipment must be prevented. ES values less than 0.5 are generally considered to be lower explosion hazards, and non-rated electrical equipment in those atmospheres is acceptable.

In January 2009, Hoeganaes submitted samples for explosibility testing. Although several samples were determined to be explosible, the ES values were low, precluding the need for classified electrical installations in the Hoeganaes facility. The CSB tested iron dust samples and found an explosion severity ratio of 0.01 to 0.1, significantly less than the ratio that would require classified equipment under existing codes.

4.4.2.2 Flammable Gases

Test results on the iron samples in the vicinity of the Hoeganaes incidents did not require the installation of classified electrical services. However, the flammable hydrogen in the band furnaces did. NFPA 497, *Recommended Practice for the Classification of Flammable Liquids, Gases, or Vapors and of Hazardous (Classified) Locations for Electrical Installations in Chemical Process Areas*, lists hydrogen as a Class I flammable gas. Areas with Class I materials are further classified as Division 2 if the material is normally contained inside the equipment, or Division 1 if the material is normally present in flammable concentrations outside the equipment, such as during maintenance. Because hydrogen normally vents into the work area at one end of the annealing furnace, the area around the annealing furnace should have been designated as Class I Division 1, and the electrical equipment in that area designed, installed, and maintained to meet those recommendations.

Moreover, the standard states that if no physical boundary surrounds a Division 1 area, the transitional area between Division 1 and an unclassified area is designated as Division 2. In addition, because the hydrogen piping system includes potential leak points, such as valves and flanges, these areas should have been designated as Class I Division 2. As such, large areas in the annealing building would be required to have Class I Division 1 or Class I Division 2 electrical service installed.

Despite these classifications and their recommendations, the CSB observed inappropriate electrical installations, including large electrical cabinets that were open to the atmosphere and that had significant iron dust accumulations, incomplete conduit, and regular 110-volt cord-plug outlets instead of ignition-proof electrical devices approved by the NEC for Class I atmospheres.

4.4.3 INTERNATIONAL FIRE CODE

The International Fire Code (IFC) establishes minimum requirements for fire protection and prevention systems. The International Code Council (ICC), a membership association responsible for developing safety codes in residential and commercial buildings, publishes the IFC. Chapter 13 of the IFC, "Combustible Dust-Producing Operations," (2006 edition) briefly addresses the prevention of ignition sources and housekeeping for areas where combustible dust is generated, stored, manufactured, or handled.[30] The IFC also references several NFPA standards, such as NFPA 484, but language in section 1304 is vague as to whether the compliance with the listed NFPA standards is mandatory or voluntary. The IFC authorizes the authority having jurisdiction, such as the fire department or municipality, to enforce "applicable provisions" of these NFPA standards; the word "authorizes" does not carry the same weight as "shall enforce" and might be interpreted as a discretionary rather than mandatory code requirement.

Companies are required to comply with the IFC only if promulgated through local, state, or federal regulations.[31] The State of Tennessee Division of Fire Prevention and the City of Gallatin both adopted the 2006 version of the IFC into their codes. Though the general precautions for housekeeping and ignition sources are required through code adoption of the IFC, the noted

---

[30]"Combustible Dust-Producing Operations" is located in Chapter 22 of the IFC 2012 edition.

[31]In a previous investigation of a serious dust explosion at West Pharmaceutical Services in North Carolina in 2003, the CSB recommended that the state require mandatory compliance with the detailed provisions of the relevant NFPA dust standard (NFPA 654) rather than the much briefer and less prescriptive requirements of IFC Chapter 13.

NFPA standards could be interpreted as voluntary. The Tennessee Fire Code specifically declares that the state does not enforce "optional or recommended" standards or practices.

Practices at the Hoeganaes facility did not conform with the requirements set forth in Chapter 13 of the IFC. The code prohibits devices using an open flame and the use of spark-producing equipment in areas with combustible dust. It also states that accumulated combustible dust will be kept to a minimum inside buildings. However, adhering to the much more detailed design and engineering requirements of NFPA 484 would have further reduced the likelihood that the three serious incidents would have occurred.

At the time of the 2011 flash fire incidents, the Hoeganaes facility was operating under the provisions of the 2006 IFC. The GFD has the authority to inspect facilities against the IFC, issue violations, and stop-work orders if buildings or operations are declared unsafe based on the code's provisions. All construction and design provisions apply to new or existing structures if, in the opinion of the code official, a distinct hazard to life or property exists. All administrative, operational, and maintenance provisions apply to new and existing conditions and operations.

For the City of Gallatin, the fire chief is responsible for enforcement of the IFC. CSB investigators reviewed the GFD's inspection history at the Hoeganaes facility. The fire department conducted three inspections in the previous 12 years, in 1999, 2002, and 2011. The 2011 inspection was performed just two weeks prior to the May 27, 2011, incident. The report for this inspection documented observations at the facility related to fire suppression and emergency egress, but did not mention combustible dust hazards even after the January and March 2011 incidents. The CSB found no evidence that the GFD inspected Hoeganaes against the provisions of the 2006 IFC for the hazards associated with combustible metal dust, electrical installation, and operations that use flammable gases.

4.5 REGULATORY OVERSIGHT

4.5.1 OSHA

4.5.1.1 Combustible Dust

In 2006, following three catastrophic dust explosions that claimed 14 lives in 2003, the CSB issued its *Combustible Dust Hazard Study*. The study identified 281 dust fires and explosions in the U.S. between 1980 and 2005 that resulted in 119 fatalities and 718 injures.

The absence of an OSHA comprehensive combustible dust standard was a key finding in the 2006 study and resulted in a CSB recommendation to OSHA to initiate rulemaking for a general industry combustible dust standard. The recommendation remains "open-acceptable"[32] as of the publication of this report.

A significant reduction in grain dust incidents resulted from a prior dust regulation enacted by OSHA for grain handling facilities. In 1987, OSHA promulgated a grain facilities standard in response to a series of major grain dust explosions. A 2003 OSHA analysis of grain dust incidents showed that fatalities dropped 60 percent after the regulation was enacted.

Another recommendation from the 2006 *CSB Combustible Dust Study* was for OSHA to develop a national special emphasis program[33] (SEP) to address dust in industry while the comprehensive standard was being developed. In October 2007, OSHA initiated a Combustible Dust National Emphasis Program (NEP) to target industries that generate, store, or handle combustible dusts. The program provides guidance to OSHA inspectors about how to apply

---

[32]In 2009, the CSB voted to change the status of the OSHA recommendation to "open-acceptable" after OSHA initiated an advance notice of proposed rulemaking (ANPR) for the combustible dust regulation.

[33]SEPs and NEPs are not regulations but rather are enforcement tools that allow OSHA to focus resources on inspections.

existing safety statutes or standards, such as the General Duty Clause (OSH Act 5(a)(1)) and the Walking-Working Surfaces standard (29 CFR 1910.22), to facilities with combustible dust.

Although the scope of the NEP applies to various types of combustible dusts including metal dusts at Hoeganaes, only those facilities assigned to particular North American Industry Classification System (NAICS) codes are specifically targeted for inspections by OSHA under the NEP. These NAICS codes classify facilities by primary business activity. If a facility that handles combustible dust is not included in the NAICS code list, OSHA can initiate an NEP inspection only as a result of a complaint, referral, or occupational injury. The NAICS code for the Hoeganaes Gallatin facility (331111, Iron and Steel Mills) is not included in the list of industries targeted by the NEP, although similar industries that handle metals are. According to the U.S. Census Bureau 2007 Economic Census, there were 352 facilities in the Iron and Steel Mills industry code (331111) employing over 106,000 workers.

The CSB 2006 dust study found that 20 percent of documented dust incidents from 1980 to 2005 occurred in the metals industry. During that period, the CSB documented three iron dust incidents that resulted in three fatalities and four injuries. One of those documented incidents occurred at the Hoeganaes Gallatin facility in 1996 when iron powder caught fire in a dust collector and one worker received a smoke inhalation injury.

In February 2008, a catastrophic sugar dust explosion at Imperial Sugar killed 14 and injured 36. A month later, OSHA revised and reissued the Combustible Dust NEP to include facilities that handle sugar. As a result, OSHA notified all facilities covered by the sugar industry codes that they were subject to inspection.

The Combustible Dust NEP is the only national OSHA program to specifically promote effective combustible dust hazard management. OSHA did not initiate rulemaking on combustible dust, as the CSB had recommended in November 2006, until April 2009. In its final report on the Imperial Sugar disaster in September 2009, the CSB recommended that OSHA "proceed expeditiously" with the new dust standard. Although OSHA issued an advance notice of proposed rulemaking (ANPR) for combustible dust in October 2009 and has since convened various stakeholder meetings, no proposed or final rule has been published.

Combustible dust fires and explosions have continued to occur at industrial facilities across the country; since issuing the 2006 CSB *Combustible Dust Study*, the CSB has recorded a number of significant combustible dust incidents. Until a combustible dust standard is enacted, the NEP remains OSHA's primary tool for addressing combustible dust in the workplace.

4.5.1.2 Process Safety Management

The Process Safety Management Standard, 29 CFR 1910.119 (PSM), is an OSHA regulation for processes that contain highly hazardous materials or significant quantities of flammables. The intent of PSM, as stated in the standard, is "preventing or minimizing the consequences of catastrophic releases of toxic, reactive, flammable, or explosive chemicals." PSM applies to processes using or producing any of 137 listed highly hazardous chemicals at or above threshold quantities and processes with flammable liquids or gases onsite in quantities of 10,000 pounds or more in one location. If applied to Hoeganaes, elements of PSM would have required practices and procedures that could have prevented or lessened the severity of the May 27, 2011 incident.

In the May 2011 incident, there was a hydrogen leak and subsequent hydrogen explosion and dust flash fires that ultimately killed three workers. The hydrogen provided to the Hoeganaes facility originates from an onsite generation and storage unit, owned and operated by a contractor on land leased from Hoeganaes. Since the hydrogen generation facility's total intended operational capacity exceeds 10,000 pounds of hydrogen, it is covered by PSM.

4.5.2 TOSHA

Tennessee is one of 24 states with a state-specific occupational safety and health plan. It develops and operates its own safety and health programs with approval from federal OSHA.

In November 2011, TOSHA issued citations to the Hoeganaes Gallatin Facility for the May 27, 2011, incident. Hoeganaes received 15 OSHA PSM Standard violations related to the hydrogen system. OSHA concluded that the company lacked appropriate procedures to ensure mechanical integrity of the hydrogen piping, failed to develop an emergency response plan for leak detection and response, and did not perform a hazard assessment on the hydrogen process.

Although the Combustible Dust NEP encourages but does not require state plans to adopt the NEP, Tennessee OSHA adopted the dust NEP in March 2008.

The NEP allows OSHA Area Offices to add NAICS codes to the list of facilities targeted by the NEP. However, TOSHA has not added the NAICS code that includes Hoeganaes as of the issuance of this study.

4.5.3 METAL DUST AWARENESS

Since Hoeganaes has been in operation, several opportunities have arisen to increase awareness and address metal dust issues at the facility through technical literature, audits, inspections, and regulatory oversight. These resources have not been effectively used by Hoeganaes. Gaps in codes and regulations, inadequate inspections, and poor hazard recognition all contributed to the three incidents at the Gallatin facility.

Table 4 lists a timeline of events from 1956 to the present related to combustible metal dust and the lack of effective controls at Hoeganaes until the third incident in May 2011.

TABLE 4

Timeline of metal dust
publications, oversight,
and opportunities to
address metal dust
hazards in industry and at
Hoeganaes.

Year	KEY MILESTONES FOR COMBUSTIBLE METAL DUST CONTROL IN INDUSTRY AND AT HOEGANAES
	Action
1946	NFPA publishes Code for the Prevention of Dust Explosions that includes general requirements for metal dusts
1958	American Chemical Society publication discusses powdered metals and iron dust explosibility
1980	Hoeganaes Gallatin facility established
1987	OSHA promulgates Grain Dust Standard, which decreases the number of explosions 44% and fatalities 60%[34]
1992	Hydrogen explosion and iron dust flash fire severely burns employee at the Hoeganaes facility in Cinnaminson, NJ
1996	Employee of Hoeganes Gallatin facility suffers smoke inhalation in dust collector fire. Metal dust ignites inside dust collector (ignited during a cutting operation)
1999	Gallatin FD inspects Hoeganaes; no mention of dust accumulations
2002	Gallatin FD inspects Hoeganaes; no mention of dust accumulations
2002	NFPA 484 is issued which addresses additional combustible metals that would include iron dust
2006	The CSB issues recommendation to OSHA to promulgate a comprehensive combustible dust standard
2006	City of Gallatin adopts International Building and Fire Codes
2007	OSHA issues Combustible Dust National Emphasis Program (NEP)
2008	Tennessee OSHA adopts federal Combustible Dust NEP (March)
2008	Tennessee OSHA inspects Hoeganaes facility. Conducts respirable metal dust sampling. Cites Hoeganaes for hearing conservation[35] (Oct.) No observation of a combustible dust hazard
2008	Allianz conducts insurance audit at Hoeganaes, recommends combustible dust testing and independent consultant (Nov.)
2009	Hoeganaes conducts combustible dust testing of three iron powder samples as recommended by 2008 Allianz audit; all three samples found to be combustible.
2010	Hoeganaes conducts combustible dust testing of 23 powdered metals; 5 of 9 iron samples found to be combustible. No substantial actions to mitigate combustible dust hazard
2011	January 31 incident; fatal combustible dust flash fire at Hoeganaes Gallatin facility
2011	March 29 incident; combustible dust flash fire at Hoeganaes Gallatin facility
2011	Gallatin FD inspects Hoeganaes, no mention of dust accumulations (May 11)
2011	May 27 incident; fatal hydrogen explosion/combustible dust flash fire at Hoeganaes Gallatin facility

4.6 METAL POWDER PRODUCERS ASSOCIATION

The Metal Powder Producers Association (MPPA) is one of six trade associations that make up the Metal Powder Industries Federation (MPIF). MPPA membership is open to manufacturers of metal powders, metal flakes, metal fibers, or non-metallic powder additives used with these materials. The stated objective of the MPPA is to "arrange for the collection and dissemination of information pertaining to the metal powder producing industries; provide technical facts, data, and standards, fundamental to metal powders and to the applications of metal powders..."[36]

[34]OSHA Office of Program Evaluation, Regulatory Review of OSHA's Grain Handling Facilities Standard (29 CFR 1910.272). February 2003.

[35]OSHA regulated program to prevent noise induced hearing loss (29 CFR 1910.35).

[36]http://www.mpif.org/aboutmpif/mppa.asp.

To achieve this, the MPPA offers a monthly newsletter and bi-annual meetings (fall and spring) to promote shared learning within the PM industry. In recent years, the spring meeting, which spotlights many safety topics, has begun focusing on the issue of combustible dust hazards in the PM industry. The MPPA has sought out external combustible dust expertise and OSHA has presented and participated in its safety meetings.

5.0 KEY FINDINGS

Over the course of investigating the events at the Hoeganaes facility, the CSB made the following key findings:

1. Significant accumulations of combustible iron powder at the Hoeganaes facility fueled fatal flash fires when lofted near an ignition source.

2. Hoeganaes facility management were aware of the iron powder combustibility hazard two years prior to the fatal flash fire incidents but did not take necessary action to mitigate the hazard through engineering controls and housekeeping.

3. Hoeganaes did not institute procedures – such as combustible gas monitoring – or training for employees to avoid flammable gas fires and explosions.

4. OSHA did not include iron and steel mills (NAICS code 331111), the industry classification code for Hoeganaes, in its Combustible Dust National Emphasis Program when it was first issued in 2007 or when it was re-issued in 2008.

5. The 2006 International Fire Code Chapter 13, *Combustible Dusts*, which was adopted by the City of Gallatin at the time of the incidents, does not clearly require jurisdictions to enforce the more comprehensive and rigorous NFPA standards for the prevention of dust fires and explosions.

6. The Tennessee Fire Code and the City of Gallatin do not enforce "optional or recommended" standards or practices of the IFC.

7. The Gallatin Fire Department inspected the Hoeganaes facility after the first two iron powder flash fires but did not cite or otherwise address combustible dust hazards present at the facility just weeks before the third fatal hydrogen explosion and dust flash fire.

8. The flame-resistant clothing (FRC) supplied by Hoeganaes to its employees did not provide any significant protection against the combustible iron dust flash fires and the hydrogen explosion that caused the fatalities.

9. GKN and Hoeganaes did not provide corporate oversight to ensure the Hoeganaes Gallatin facility was adequately managing combustible dusts prior to and throughout the succession of serious incidents at the Gallatin facility.

6.0 RECOMMENDATIONS

6.1 OSHA

2011-4-I-TN-R1
Ensure that the forthcoming OSHA Combustible Dust Standard includes coverage for combustible metal dusts including iron and steel powders.

2011-4-I-TN-R2
Develop and publish a proposed combustible dust standard for general industry within one year of the approval of this case study.

2011-4-I-TN-R3
Revise the Combustible Dust National Emphasis Program (NEP) to add industry codes for facilities that generate metal dusts (e.g., North American Industrial Classification System, NAICS, code 331111 Iron and Steel Mills, and other applicable codes not currently listed). Send notification letters to all facilities nationwide under these codes to inform them of the hazards of combustible metal dusts and NEP coverage.

6.2 INTERNATIONAL CODE COUNCIL

2011-4-I-TN-R4
Revise IFC Chapter 22[37] Combustible Dust Producing Operations; Section 2204.1 Standards, to require mandatory compliance and enforcement with the detailed requirements of the NFPA standards cited in the chapter, including NFPA 484.

6.3 TOSHA

2011-4-I-TN-R5
Revise the state-adopted Dust National Emphasis Program (NEP) to add industry codes for facilities that generate metal dusts (e.g., North American Industrial Classification System, NAICS, code 331111 Iron and Steel Mills, and other applicable codes not currently listed). Send notification letters to all facilities statewide under these codes to inform them of the hazards of combustible metal dusts and NEP coverage.

6.4 HOEGANAES

2011-4-I-TN-R6
Conduct periodic independent audits of the Hoeganaes Gallatin facility for compliance with the following NFPA standards, using knowledgeable experts, and implement all recommended corrective actions:

- NFPA 484, *Standard for Combustible Metals, Metal Powders, and Metal Dusts*
- NFPA 499, *Recommended Practice for the Classification of Combustible Dusts and of Hazardous Locations for Electrical Installations in Chemical Process Areas*
- NFPA 497, *Recommended Practice for the Classification of Flammable Liquids, Gases, or Vapors and of Hazardous (Classified) Locations for Electrical Installations in Chemical Process Areas*
- NFPA 2, *Hydrogen Technologies Code*
- NFPA 2113, *Standard on Selection, Care, Use, and Maintenance of Flame-Resistant Garments for Protection of Industrial Personnel Against Flash Fire*

---

[37]Combustible Dust Producing Operations, Chapter 13 of the IFC, was moved to Chapter 22 in later editions.

2011-4-I-TN-R7

Develop training materials that address combustible dust and plant-specific metal dust hazards and train all employees and contractors. Require periodic (e.g., annual) refresher training for all employees and contractors.

2011-4-I-TN-R8

Implement a preventive maintenance program and leak detection and leak mitigation procedures for all flammable gas piping and gas processing equipment.

2011-4-I-TN-R9

Develop and implement a near-miss reporting and investigation policy that includes the following at a minimum:

- Ensure facility-wide worker participation in reporting all near-miss events and operational disruptions (such as significant iron powder accumulations, smoldering fires, or unsafe conditions or practices) that could result in worker injury.

- Ensure that the near-miss reporting program requires prompt investigations, as appropriate, and that results are promptly circulated throughout the Hoeganaes Corporation.

- Establish roles and responsibilities for the management, execution, and resolution of all recommendations from near-miss investigations

- Ensure the near-miss program is operational at all times (e.g. nights, weekends, holiday shifts).

6.5 METAL POWDER PRODUCERS ASSOCIATION (MPPA)

2011-4-I-TN-R10

Communicate the findings of this report to all your members, e.g. through a safety article in an upcoming monthly newsletter.

6.6 CITY OF GALLATIN, TN

2011-4-I-TN-R11

Require all facilities covered by IFC Chapter 13 (2006 edition) to conform to NFPA standards for combustible dusts including NFPA 484.

6.7 GALLATIN FIRE DEPARTMENT

2011-4-I-TN-R12

Ensure that all industrial facilities in the City of Gallatin are inspected periodically against the International Fire Code. All facility inspections shall be documented.

2011-4-I-TN-R13

Implement a program to ensure that fire inspectors and response personnel are trained to recognize and address combustible dust hazards.

APPENDIX A: DETERMINATION OF IRON POWDER EXPLOSIBILITY FROM PRESSURE RATIO CALCULATIONS

BACKGROUND

The CSB commissioned testing of four Hoeganaes iron dust samples in a 20-L Test Chamber (ASTM Standard E1226-10, *Standard Test Method for Explosibility of Dust Clouds).* The test method states that dust explosibility can also be characterized through the calculation of a pressure ratio (PR). The pressure ratio calculation is also known as the explosibility screening test (Section 13). The 20-L test chamber records the maximum explosion pressure reached during a single deflagration test at a dust concentration of 1,000 and 2,000 g/m^3.

If PR > 2, the dust is considered explosible

If PR < 2, it is classified as "not explosible" under those test conditions and the standard goes on to caution that it is not necessarily "not combustible" and still may be capable of deflagrative combustion.

CALCULATIONS

The CSB calculated the pressure ratio based on the 20-L test results from the baghouse dust. According to E1226-10:

$$Pressure\ ratio = PR = (P_{ex,a} - \Delta P_{ignitor}) / P_{ignition}$$

Where:

$P_{ex,a}$ = maximum explosion pressure (bar absolute)

$\Delta P_{ignitor}$ = maximum pressure rise in chamber due to igniter = 2.5 (bar absolute)

$P_{ignition}$ = absolute pressure at the time of ignition = 0 bar gauge = 1.0123 (bar absolute)

The test value $P_{max,a}$ already corrects for the igniter pressure:

$$P_{max,a} = (P_{ex,a} - \Delta P_{ignitor})$$

$P_{max,a}$ values obtained from 20L testing of Hoeganaes dust:

$P_{max,a}$	DUST CONCENTRATION
3.1 bar gauge	1,000 g/m^3
3.8 bar gauge	2,000 g/m^3

Convert bar gauge to bar absolute:

0 *bar gauge* = 1.0125 *bar absolute*

3.1 *bar gauge* + 1.01325 = 4.1 *bar absolute*

3.8 *bar gauge* + 1.0125 = 4.8 *bar absolute*

The equation reduces to:

$$PR = P_{max,a} / P_{ignition}$$

Thus:

$$PR_{1,000} = 4.1/1.01325$$

$$\boldsymbol{PR_{1,000} = 4.0}$$

$$PR_{2,000} = 4.8/1.01325$$

$$\boldsymbol{PR_{2,000} = 4.7}$$

The pressure ratios at 1,000 and 2,000 g/m³ are both **greater than 2** and the iron dust sample is considered **explosible** based on ASTM E1226.

APPENDIX B: DETERMINATION OF IRON POWDER CLASSIFICATION FROM EXPLOSION SEVERITY CALCULATION

BACKGROUND

The CSB commissioned testing of four Hoeganaes iron dust samples in a 20-L Test Chamber (ASTM Standard E1226-10, *Standard Test Method for Explosibility of Dust Clouds*). OSHA cites the National Materials Advisory Board (NMAB) 353-3-80, *Classification of Combustible Dusts in Accordance with the National Electric Code*, for the determination of a Class II combustible dust location. The NMAB 353-3-80 states that Class II dusts can be characterized through the calculation of an explosion severity (ES). According to the NMAB 353-3-80:

> If ES > 0.5, the dust is considered an appreciable explosion hazard that requires suitable electrical equipment for Class II locations.

CALCULATIONS

The CSB calculated the pressure ratio based on the 20-L test results from the baghouse dust. According to NMAB 353-3-80:

$$Explosion\ Severity = ES = \frac{P_{max\ (sample)} \times \frac{\partial P}{\partial t}_{max\ (sample)}}{P_{max\ (reference\ dust)} \times \frac{\partial P}{\partial t}_{max\ (reference\ dust)}}$$

Where:

P_{max} = maximum explosion pressure, (bar gauge)

$\frac{\partial P}{\partial t}_{max\ (reference\ dust)}$ = maximum rate of pressure rise, (bar gauge per second)

Reference dust = Pittsburgh coal dust

P_{max} values obtained from 20L testing of Hoeganaes dust:

DUST SAMPLE	P_{max}	$\partial P/\partial t_{max}$
Hoeganaes Baghouse	3.5 bar gauge	68 bar gauge per second
Pittsburgh Coal	7.3 bar gauge	426 bar gauge per second

Thus:

$$ES = \frac{(3.5 \; bar \; gauge) \times (68 \; \frac{bar \; gauge}{s})}{(7.3 \; bar \; gauge) \times (426 \; \frac{bar \; gauge}{s})}$$

$$ES = \frac{238}{3,110}$$

$$ES = 0.077$$

The explosion severity of the baghouse dust is **less than** 0.5 and the iron dust sample is **not considered a Class II combustible dust.**